ANOTHER DIMENSION 2

THE LITTLE BOOK

21st CENTURY PUBLISHING, INC.

Copyright © 1994 by 21st Century Publishing, Inc.
Images copyright © 1994 Otherworld Artyfax
Copyright © 1994 Small Wonders, copyright © 1994 Ultragrafix
All rights reserved.

ISBN 0-9640954-1-6

Written Text, Layout and Cover Design by Steve Perry
Printed in the U.S.A. by Lithographix, Inc.

An introduction

Welcome to the expanding world of stereographic 3D. Brian Small, Ryan Jones and Glenn Canady have been busy creating 47 new images. This time they decided to experiment and try some new things while still giving everyone the same high quality they are used to. We think that you will agree that they have been very successful and these images will soon win your appreciation as they have ours.

Following the first book, these artists received many inquiries from individuals and corporations to make images for special occasions or promotional materials. Since the artists have completed the images for this book they can begin to handle this backlog of commission work. These inquiries are interesting because you never know what someone is going to ask us to create next.

Every week we get in more letters from 3D enthusiasts saying that the images in the "Another Dimension" books are the best in the world. Due to the competence and hard work of these artists, 21st Century Publishing expects this to be the case for some time.

Make sure you sharpen up your skills for viewing these stereograms because we are currently working with newspapers all over the country to hold contests that will give prizes to those that can report all the 3D details in stereograms.

Some papers plan to run the contest every weekend for a year. You can call the newspapers in your area (marketing department) to see if they plan to run our 3D contest. If they haven't heard about it, have them contact us directly or send their name, address and phone number to the address in the back of this book and we will contact them.

How to view these pictures in 3D

There are a number of different ways to see these images but the key to all of them is for the printed picture to be out of focus. This will allow the eyes and mind to resolve the illusion and reveal the 3D image. Just relax and let it happen. It's truly amazing when it does.

Technique One:
Look for your reflection on the cover of this book. If you can see your reflection, look at it and let the picture go blurry (out of focus). If the 2D surface of the picture is not blurry, the 3D image will not appear.

Once you have your attention on the reflection, just relax. Sometimes it takes a few minutes but we assure you it is worth your time. You will start to feel something happen. Just keep doing the the same thing and soon the image will appear.

You will find that after you see the 3D images inside for the first time it rapidly gets easier and easier. You should try all the techniques to find which one is easiest for you.

Technique Two:
Look toward the picture but do not focus on anything. Just kind of give a blank stare, then relax. After a bit you will start to "feel" something happen. The picture will start to change, when it does this just keep relaxing and doing the same thing. Your eyes will do the rest of the work when you are patient. When the image first comes in, it usually is just a piece of it. Continue to do the same relaxed stare and the rest will "pop" in.

Technique Three:
Place the picture one inch in front of your eyes. The picture will be totally blurry. Let your eyes get a little used to it. Then, without changing the focus of your eyes, slowly move the picture away from your eyes. Then stop at arms length. The picture should be blurry. If it is, just relax and go with the flow. If it is not, then start over. It will get easier.

If you have any trouble viewing these pictures, don't worry. Many of us have trouble the first time. In fact, I didn't see it until the second time I tried. Do not overdo it the first time as this is exercising parts of the eye that have not really been used before and the muscles can get tired. Try it later or the next day with a fresh new outlook.

Technique Four:
This is called the "view through" method. It is done by focusing your eyes through and behind the picture. When you do this the picture will begin to get blurry then the eye will start to adjust. Like the other techniques just relax. Once you get better at viewing these pictures this will probably be the fastest way to see the picture inside.

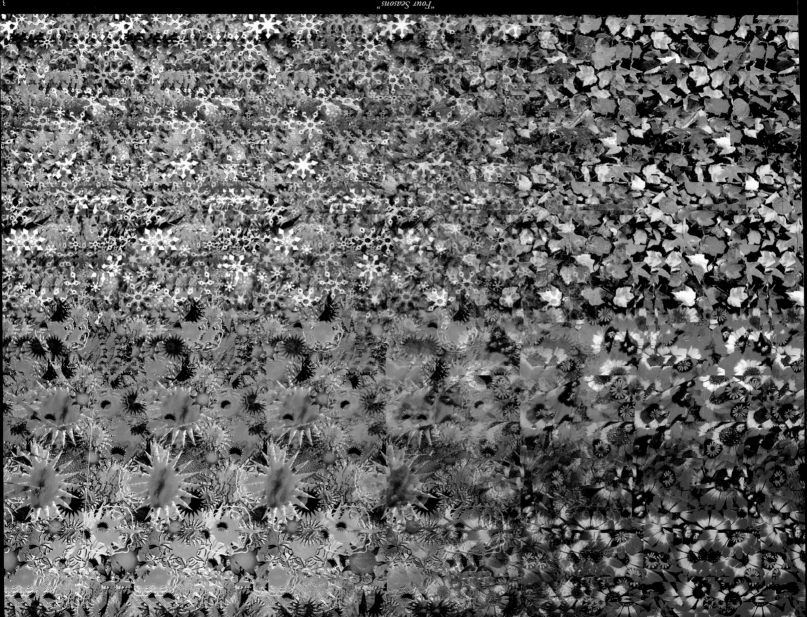
"Four Seasons"

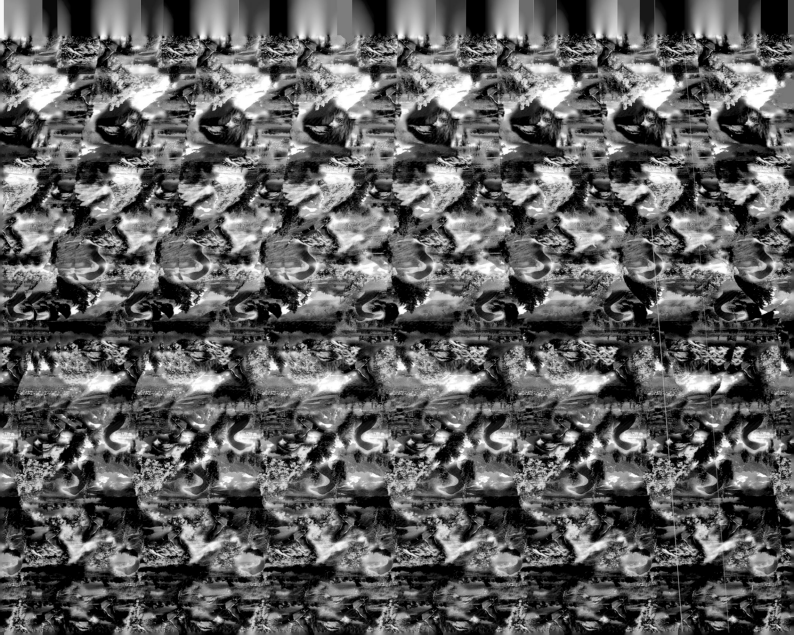

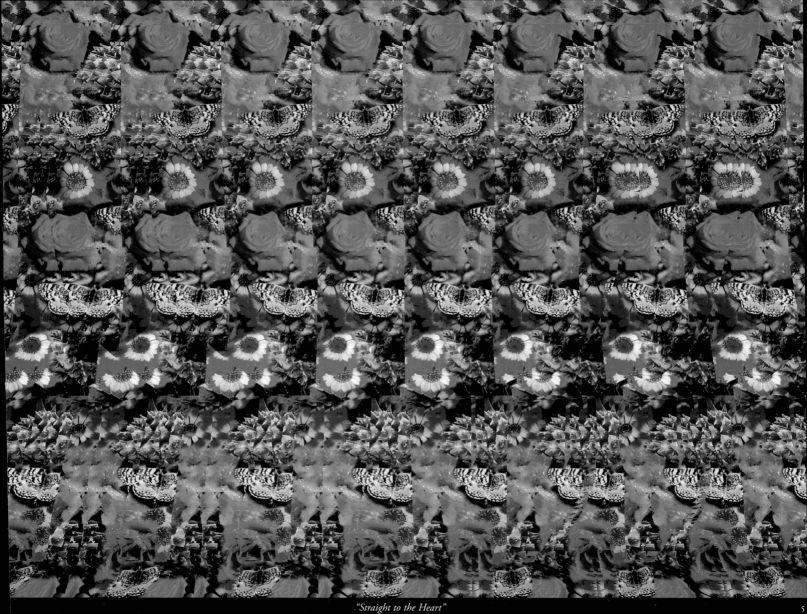

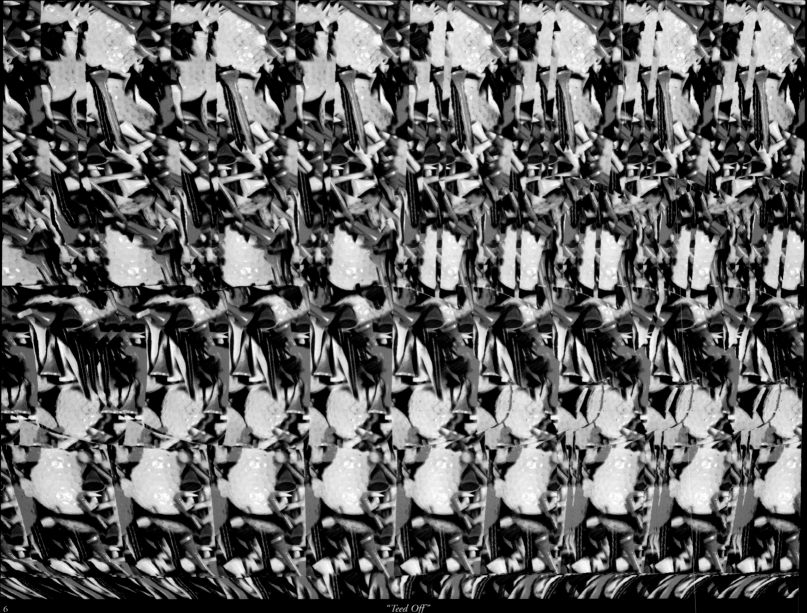

"Teed Off"

"Beethoven's Biz"

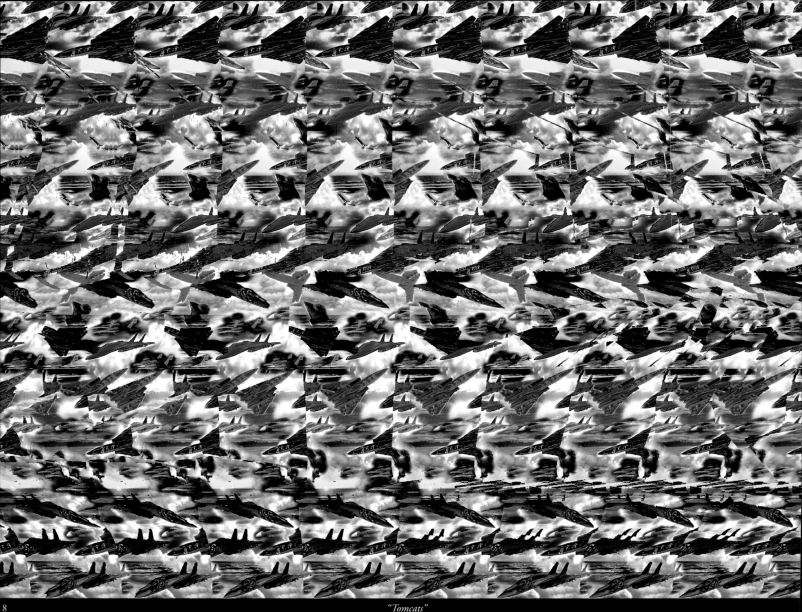

"Tomcats"

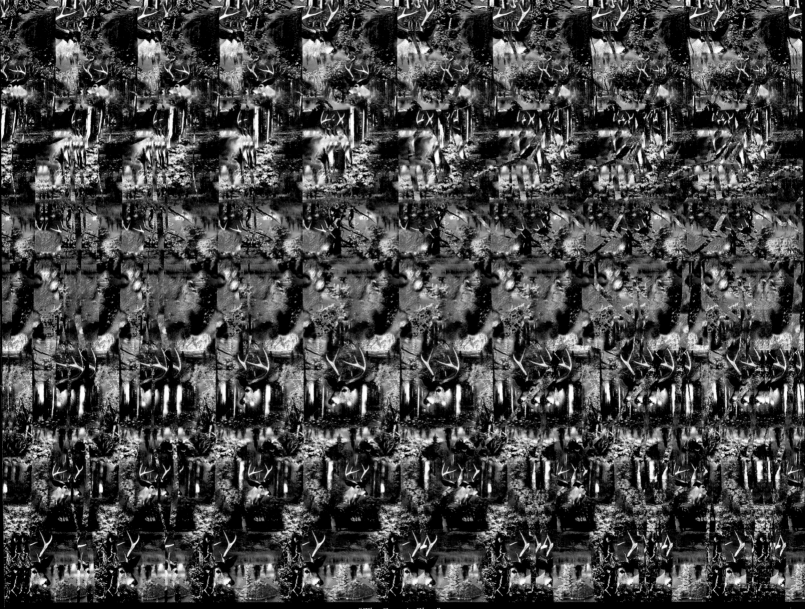

"The Coast is Clear"

"Smooth"

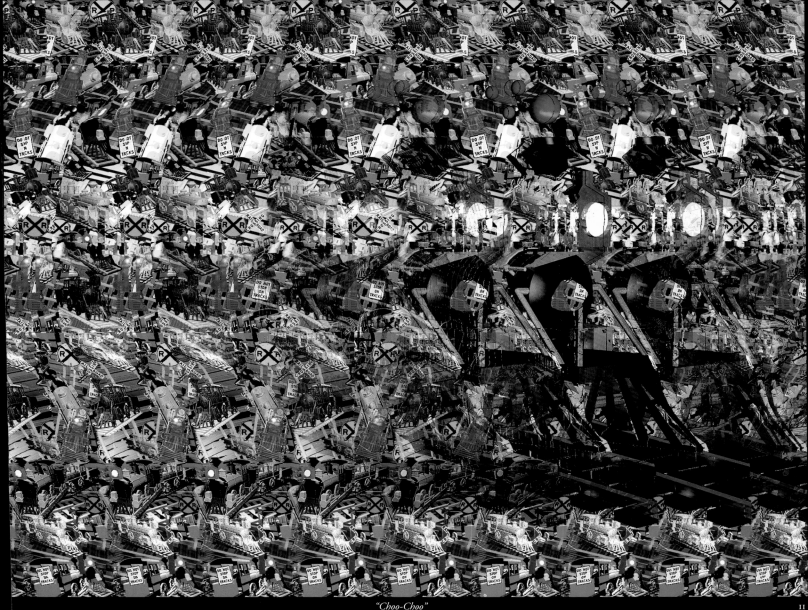

"Choo-Choo"

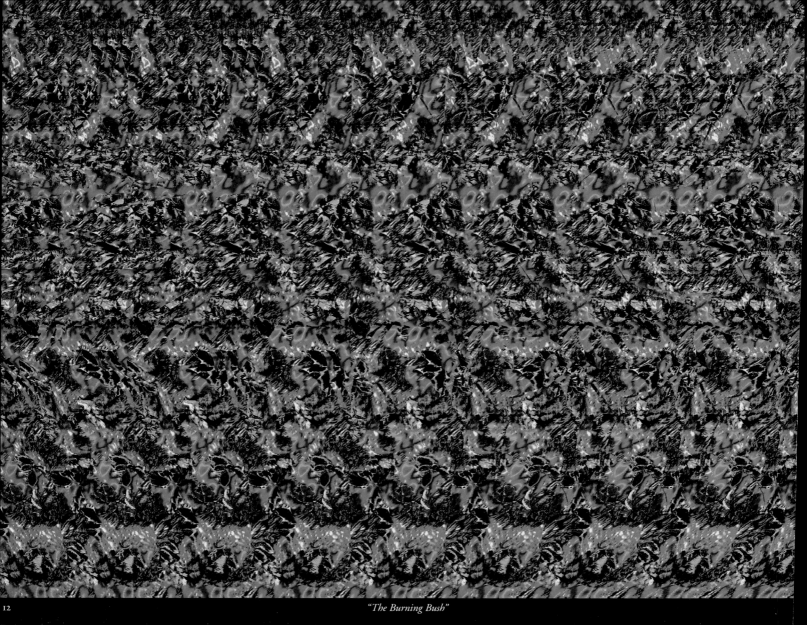

"The Burning Bush"

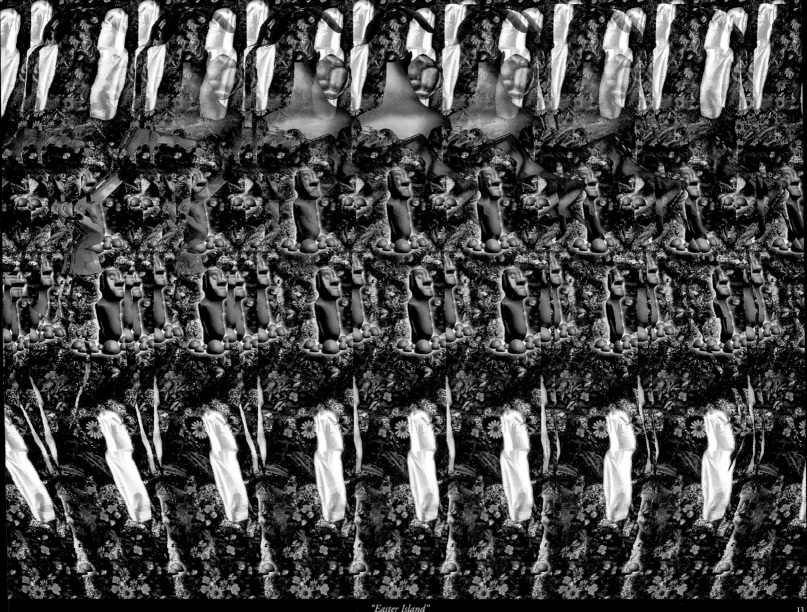

"Easter Island"

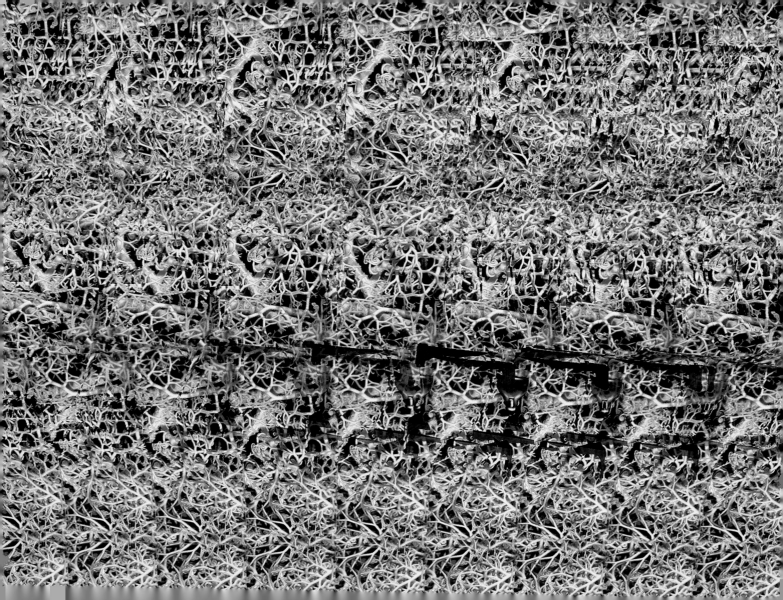

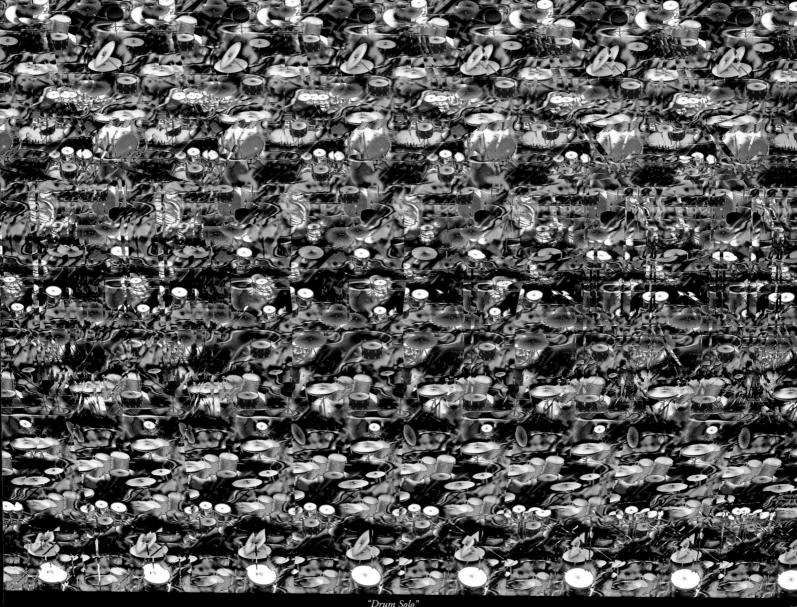

"Drum Solo"

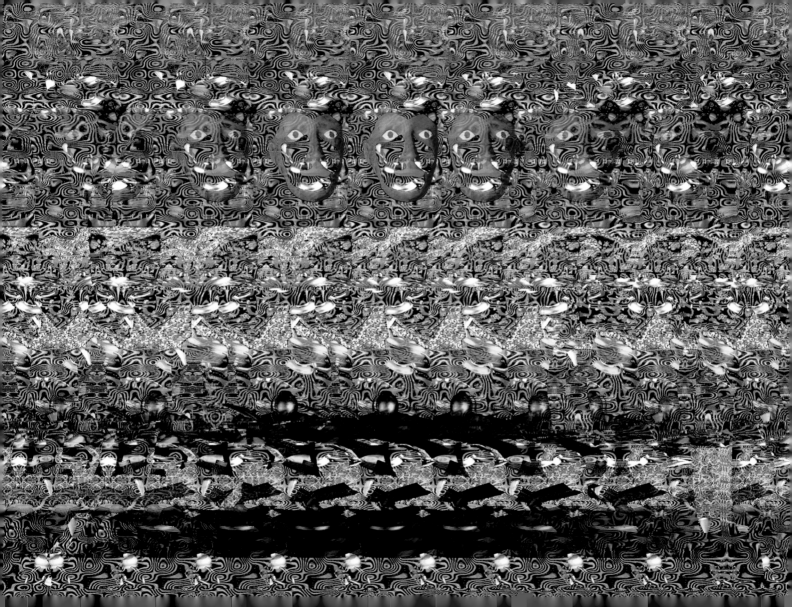

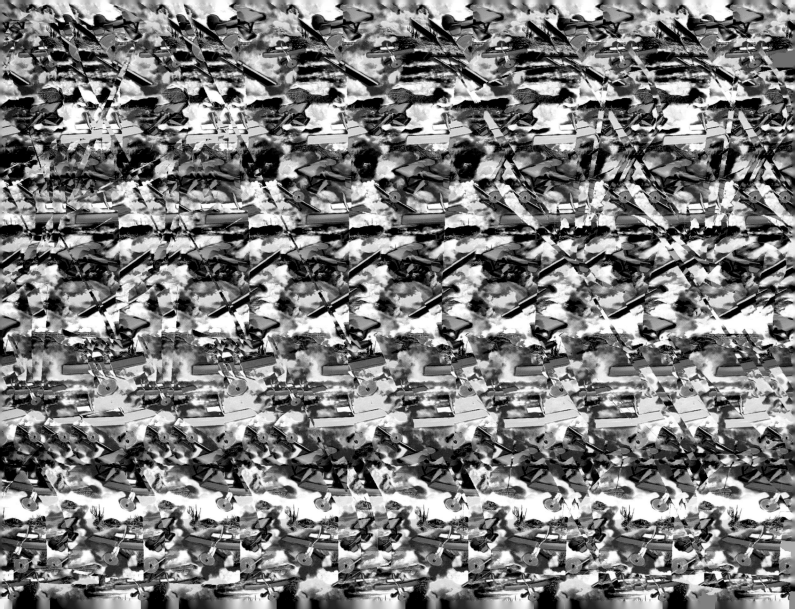

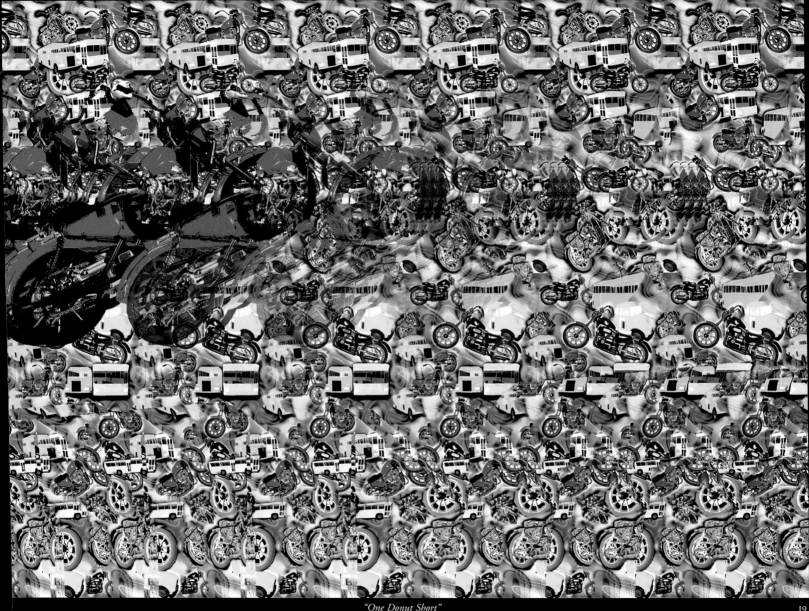

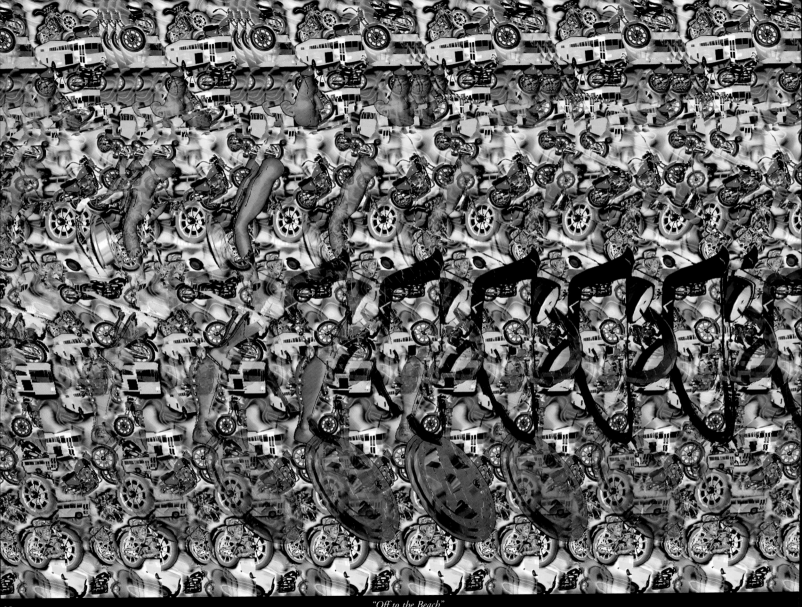

"Off to the Beach"

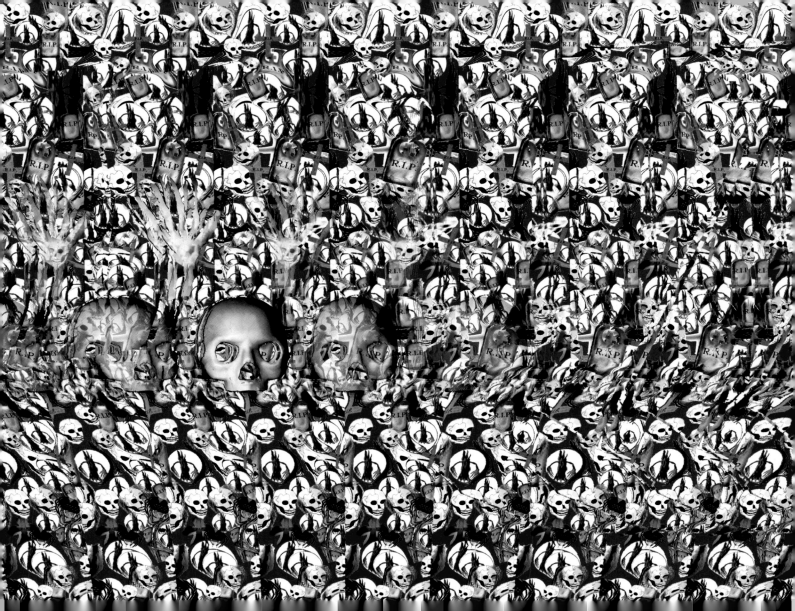

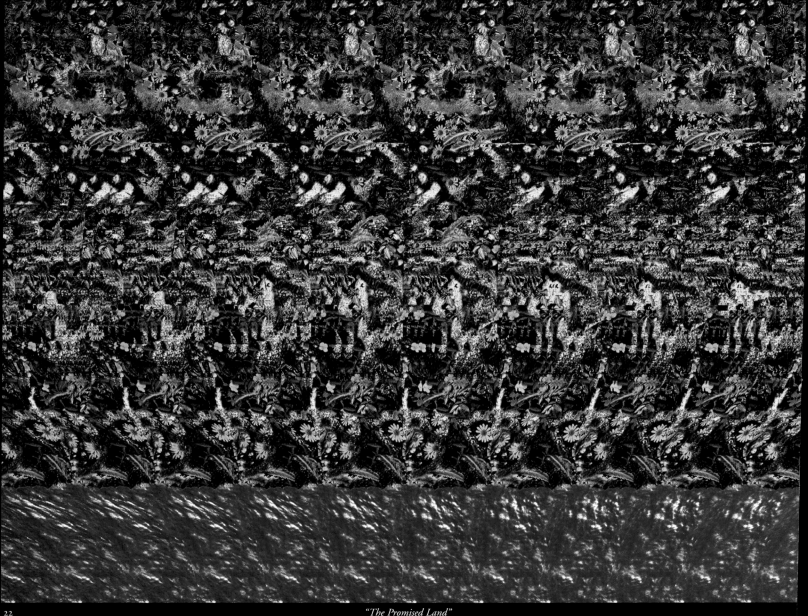

"The Promised Land"

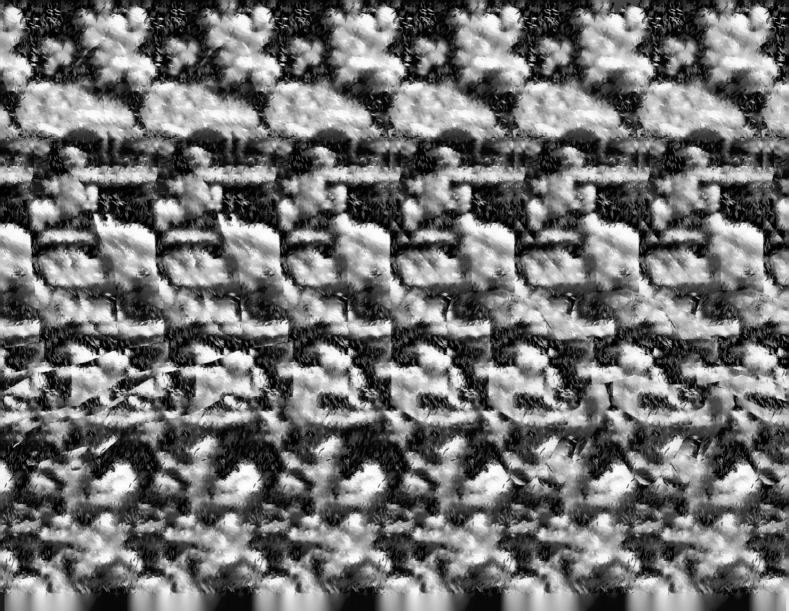

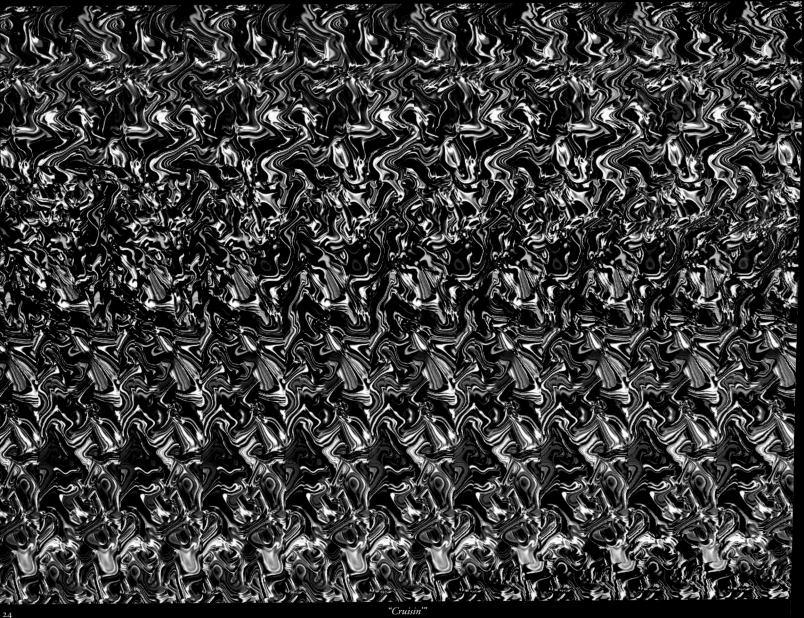

"Cruisin'"

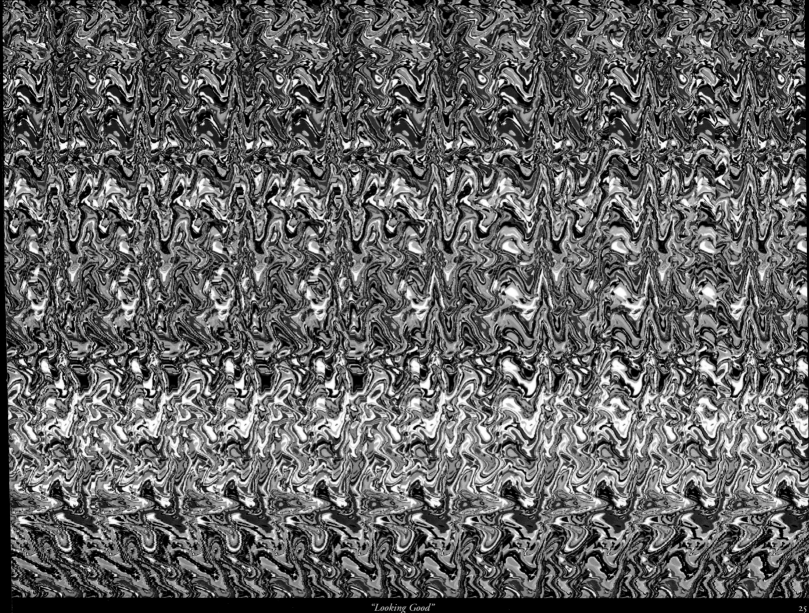

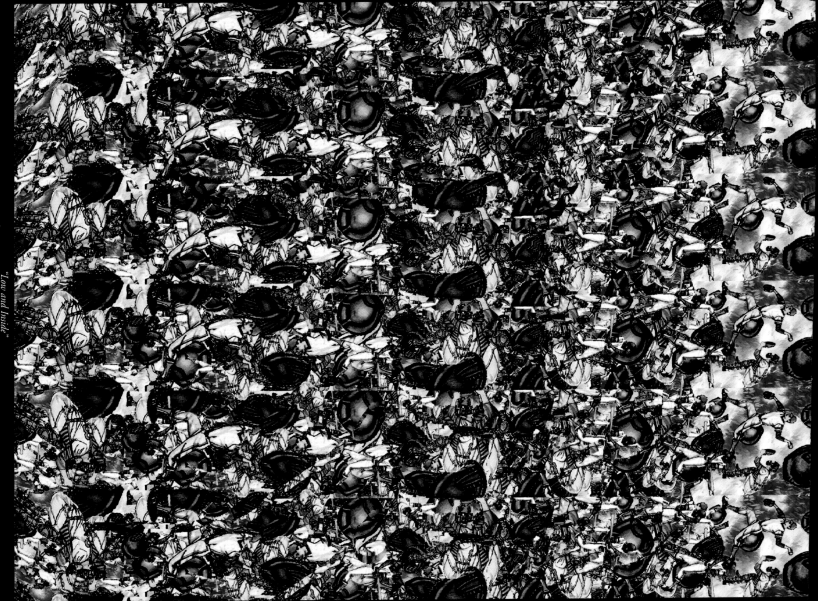

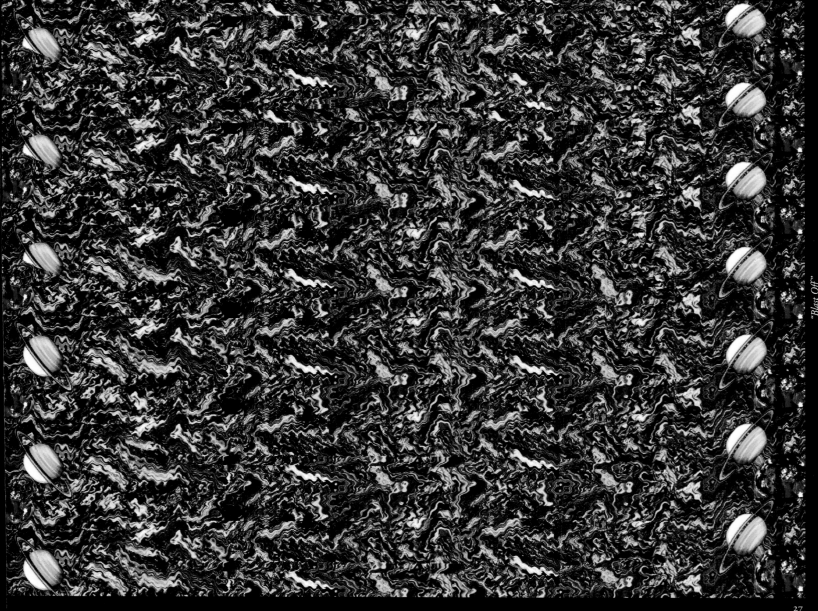

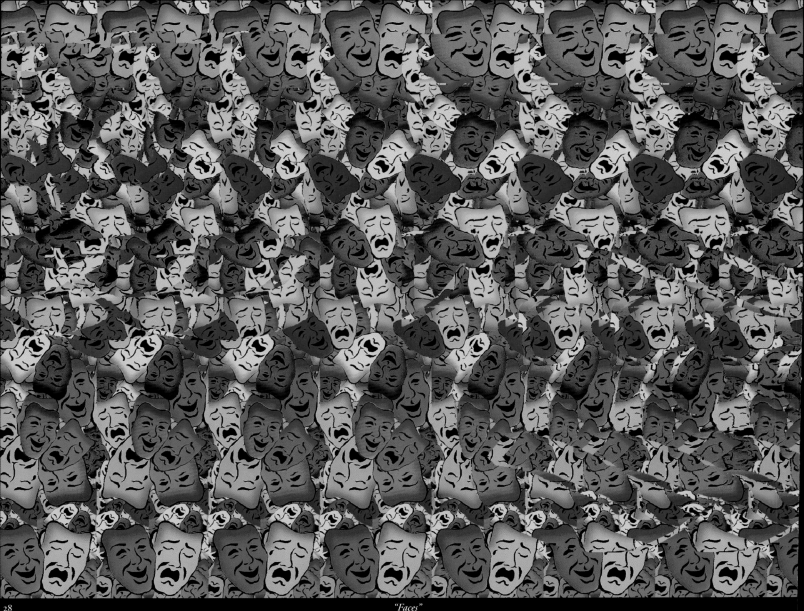

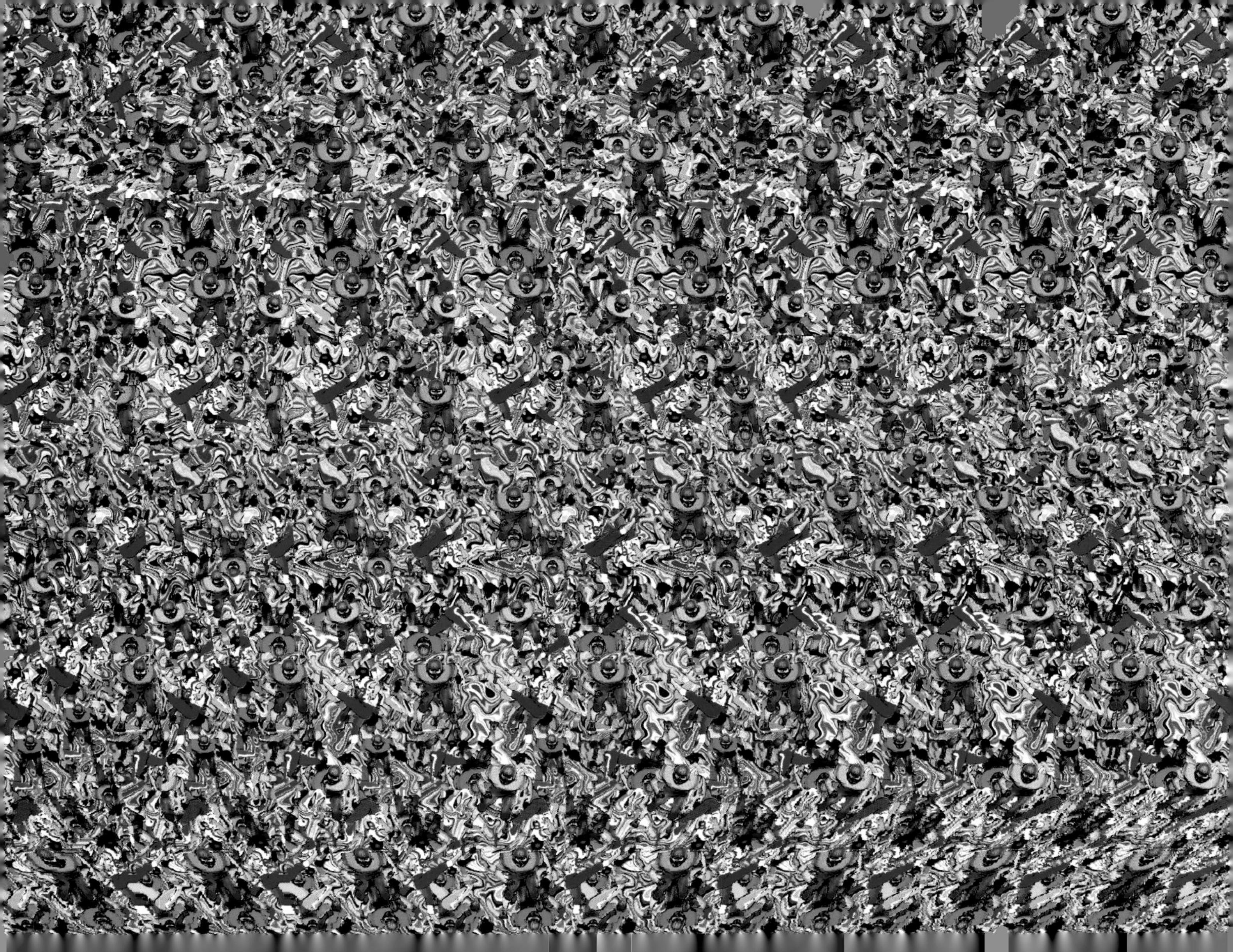

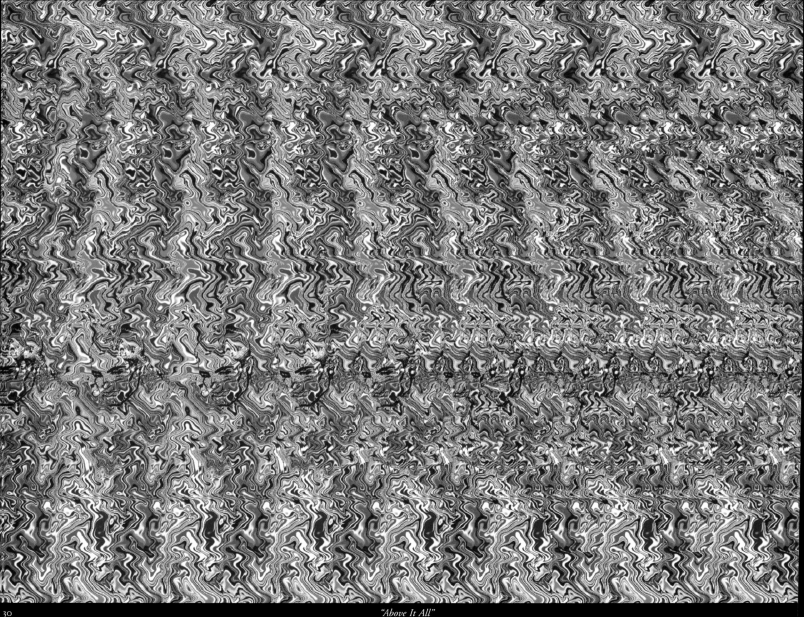

"Above It All"

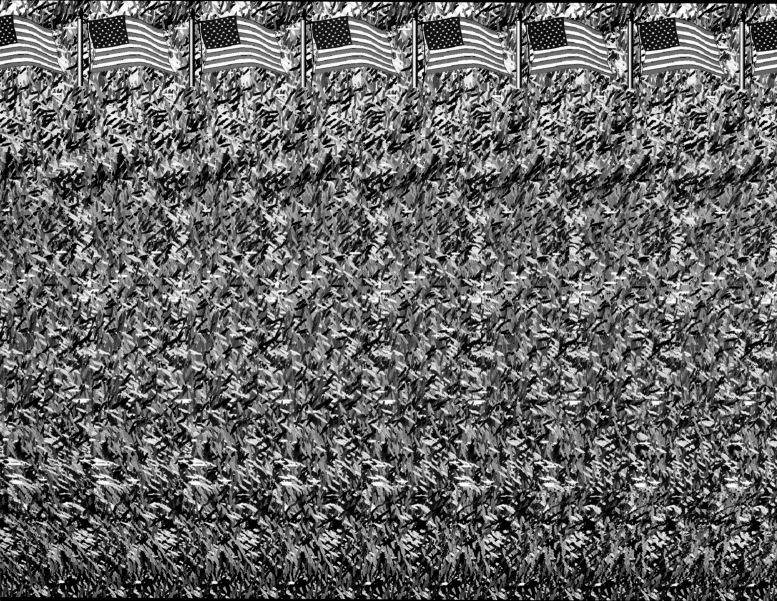

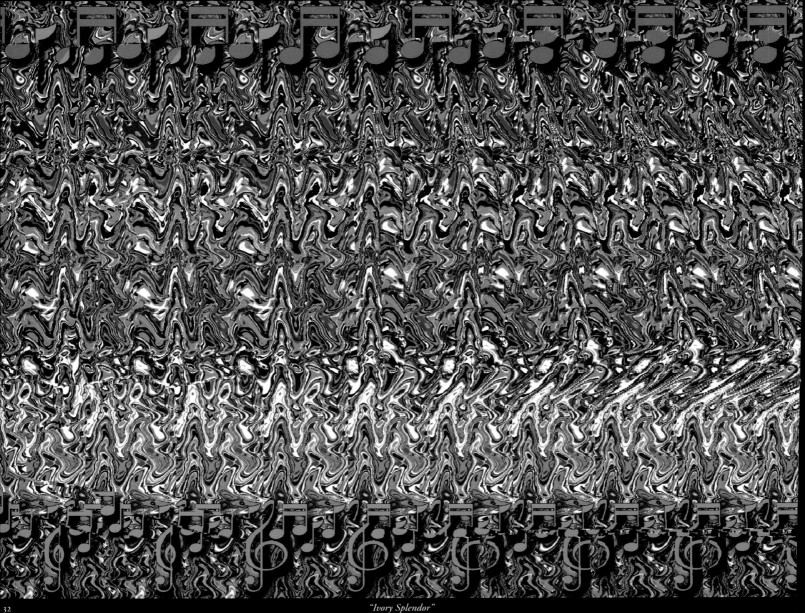

"Ivory Splendor"

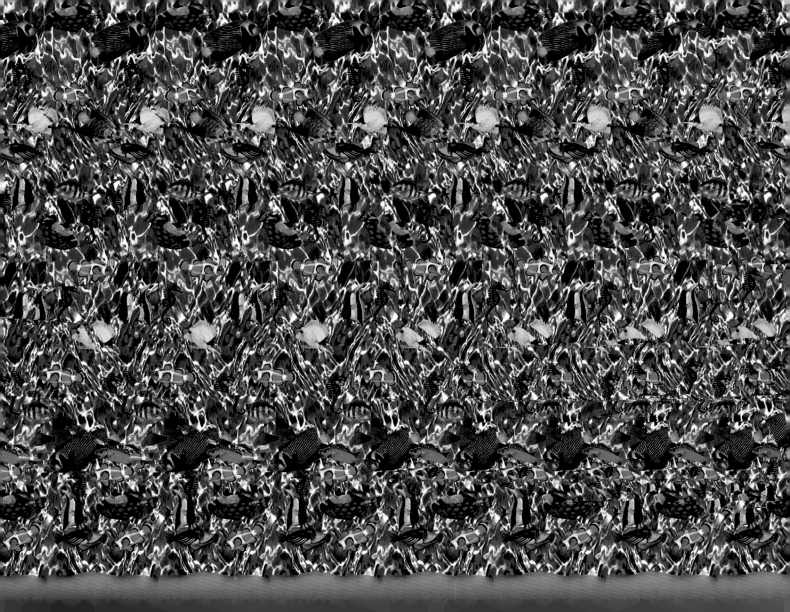

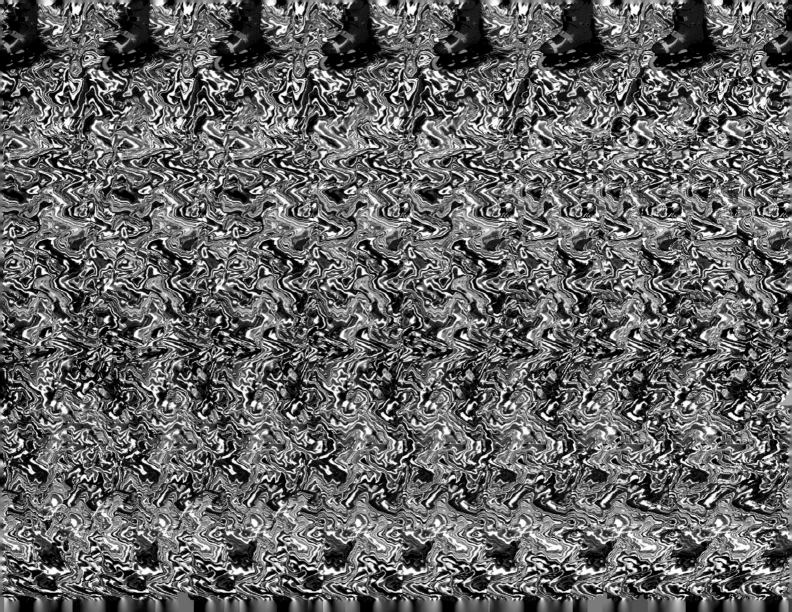

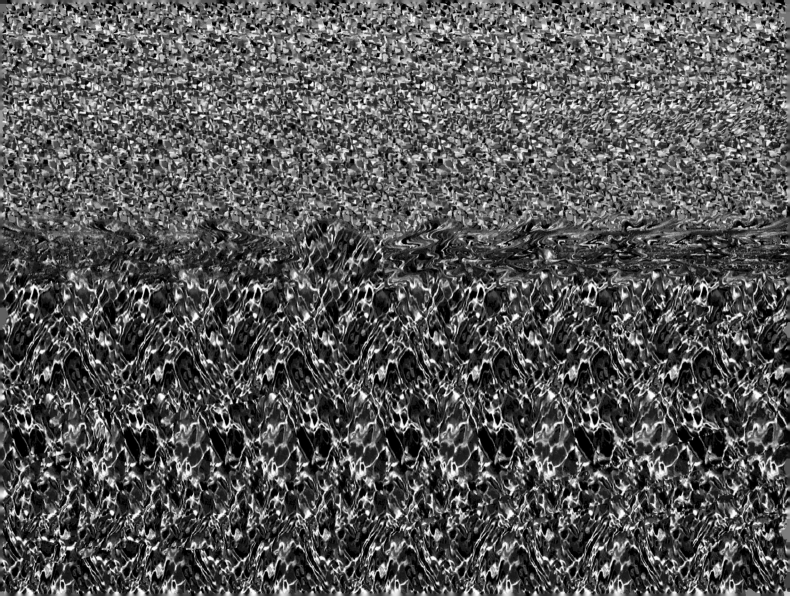

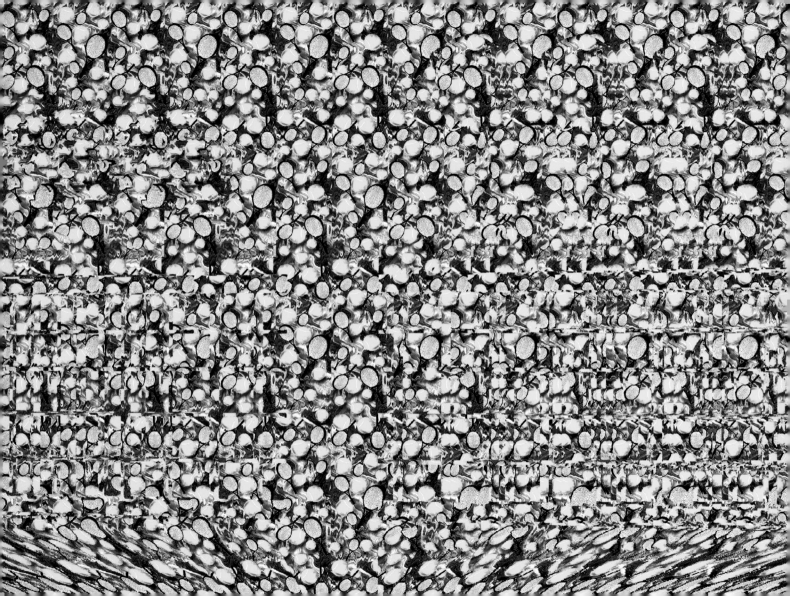

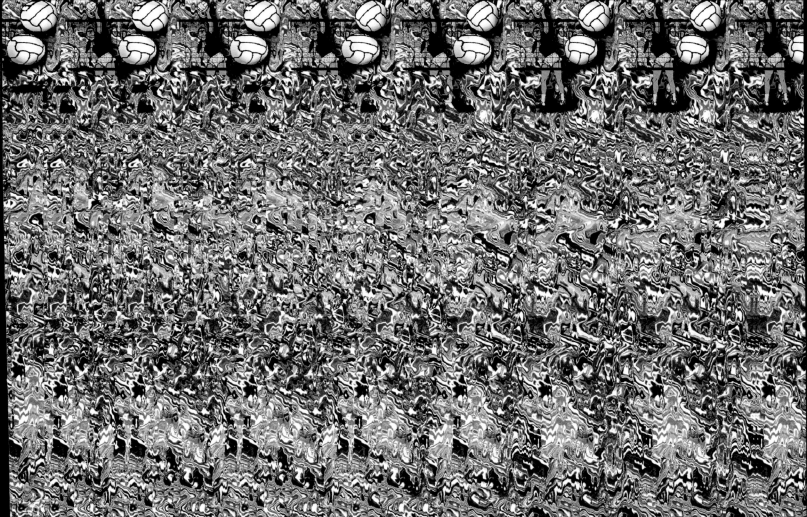

"Gotcha"

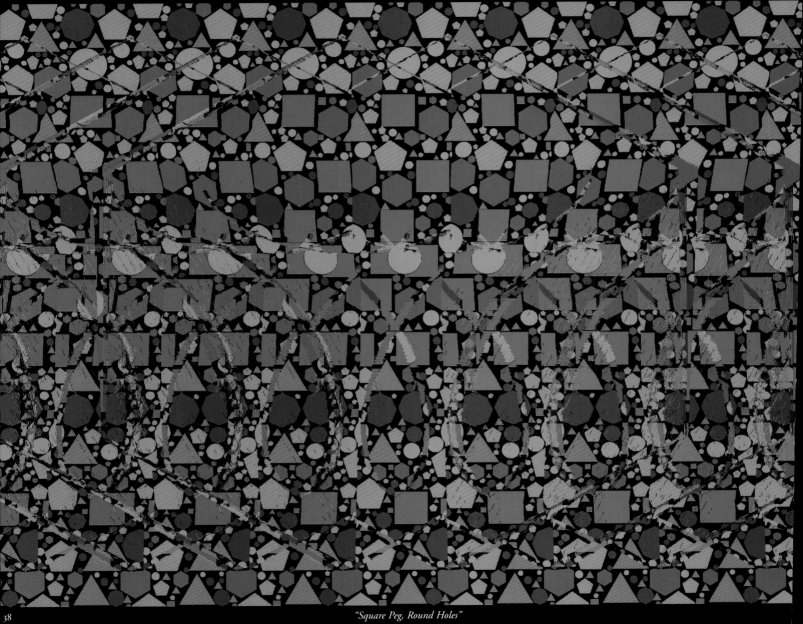

"Square Peg, Round Holes"

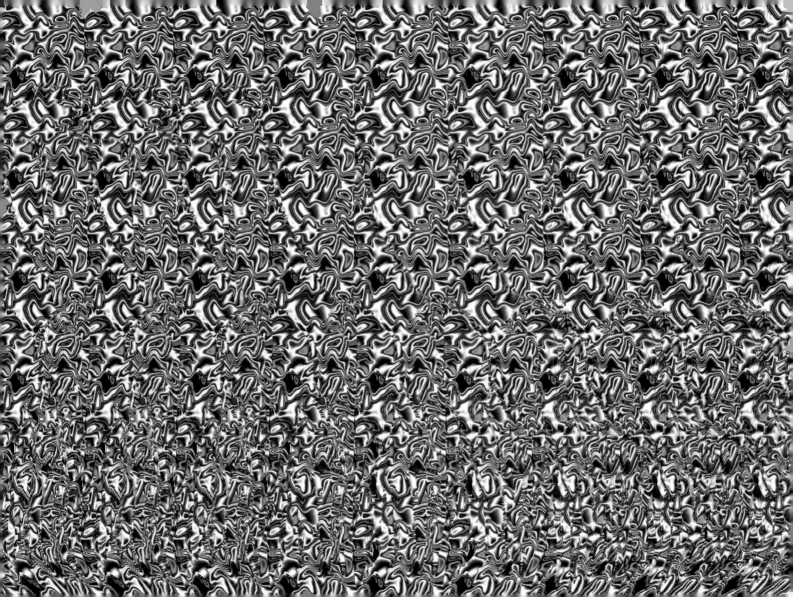

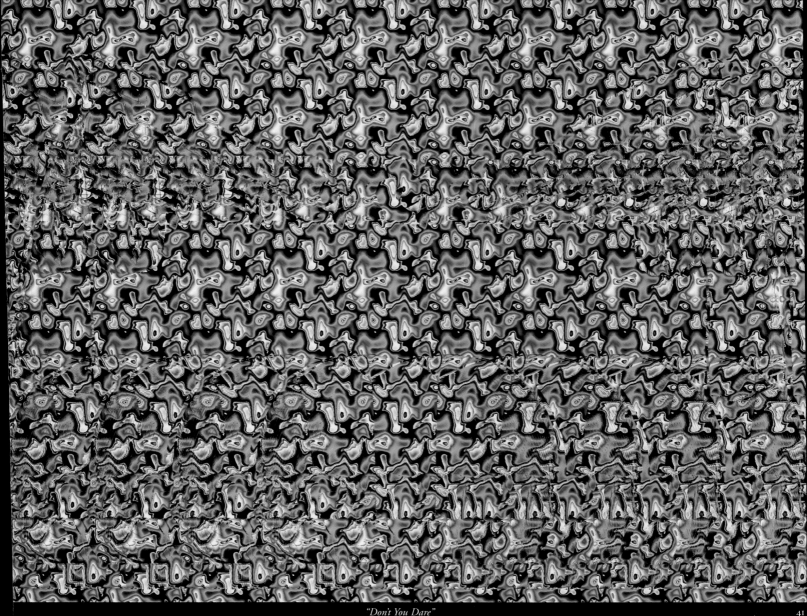

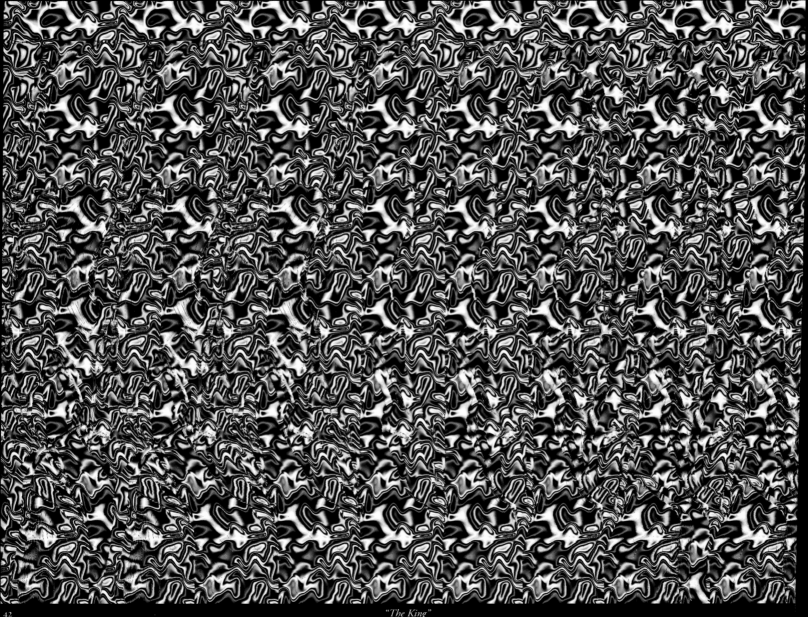

"The King"

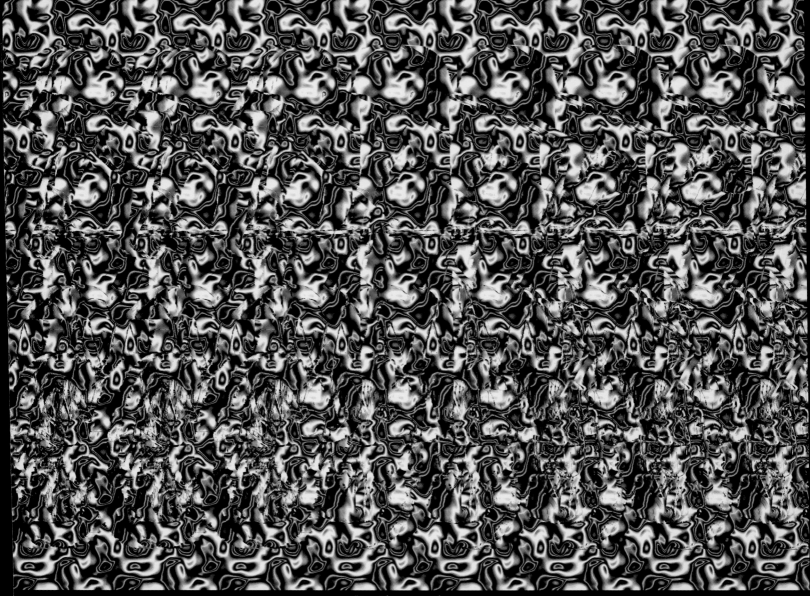

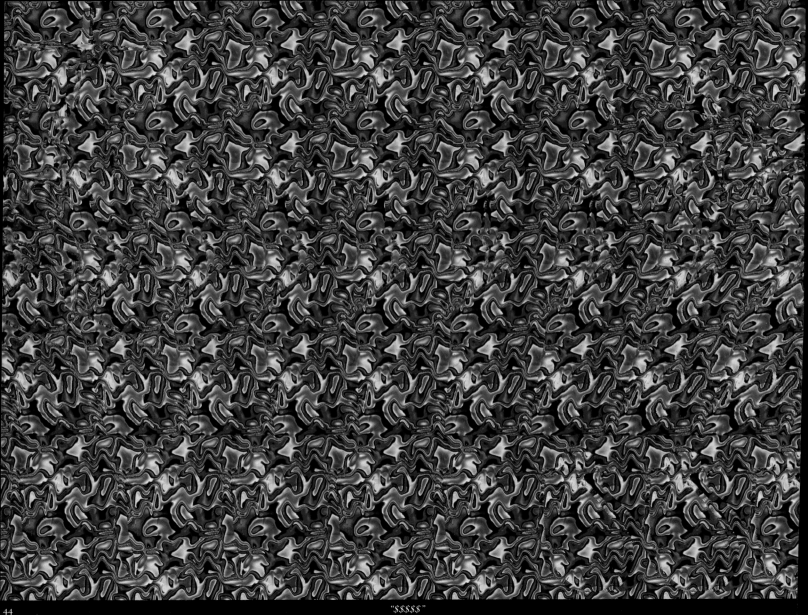

"$$$$$"

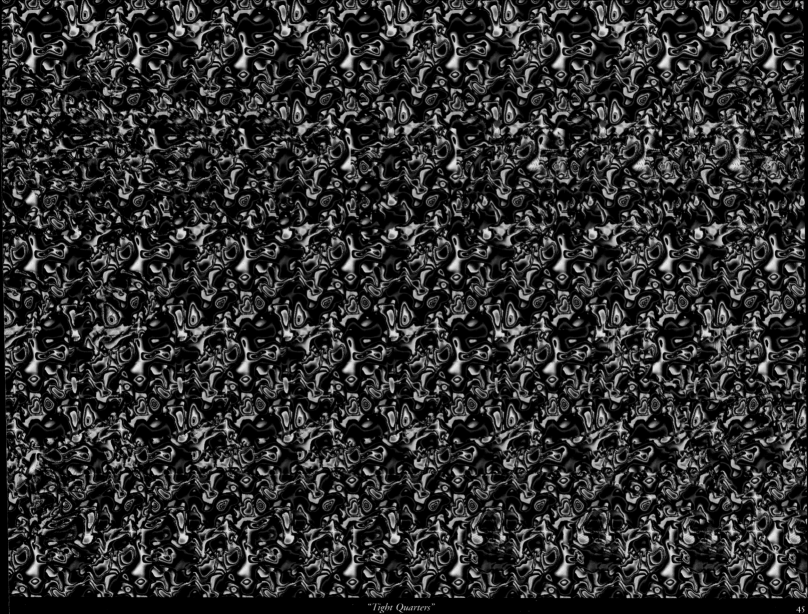

"Tight Quarters"

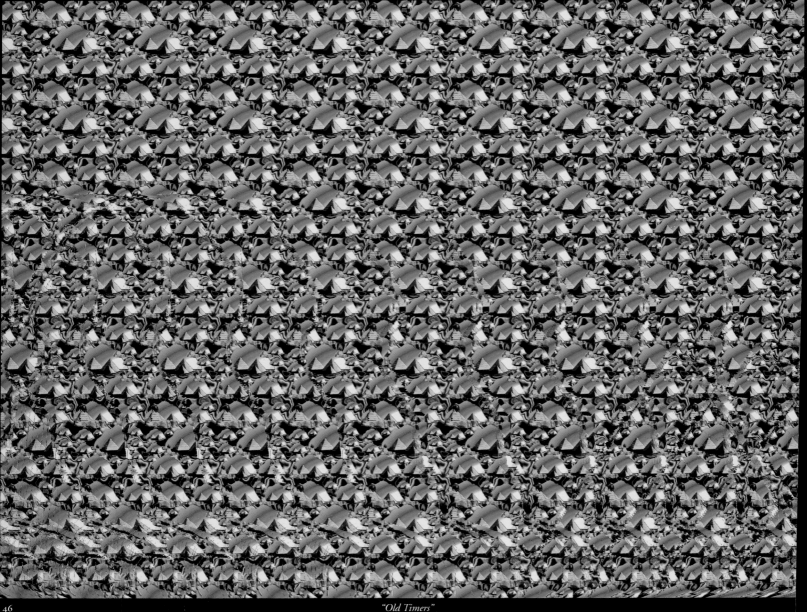

"Old Timers"

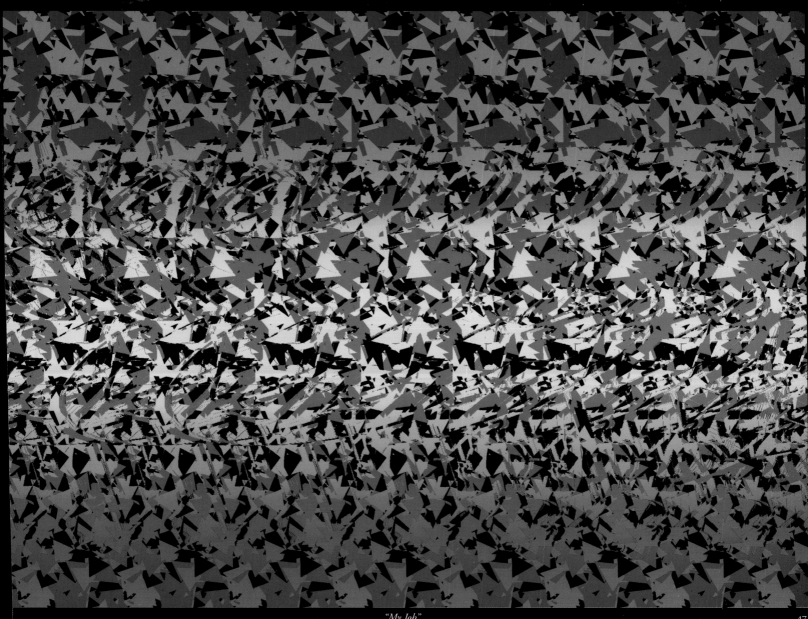

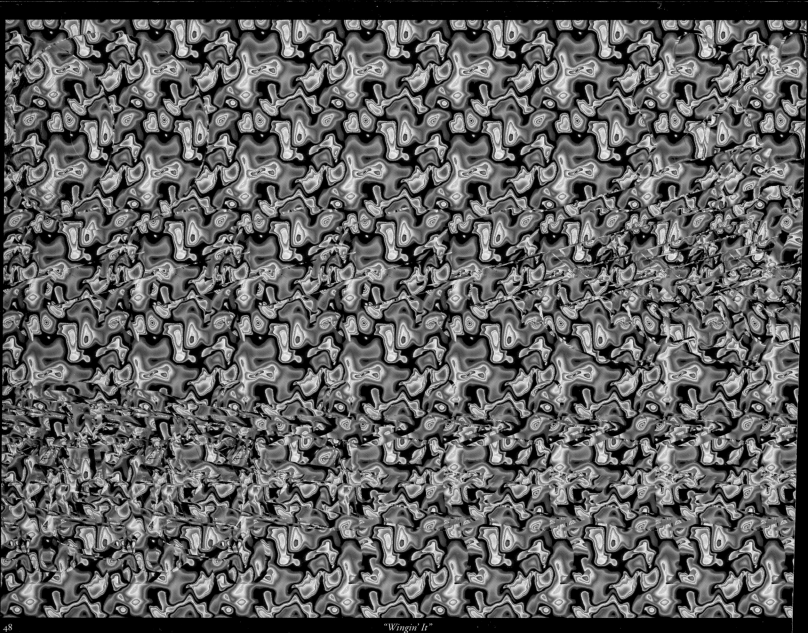

"Wingin' It"